WITHDRAWN
Damaged, Obsolete or Surplus
Jackson County Library Services

DATE DUE AUG 04

GAYLORD PRINTED IN U.S.A.

RAVES REVIEWS FOR LATER LIFE

"Extremely funny and very touching." —HOWARD KISSEL, *Daily News*

"Charmingly clever . . . immeasurably touching." —*New York Post*

"*Later Life* offers one of our best playwrights at the top of his form."
—*Variety*

A. R. GURNEY, winner of the 1987 Award of Merit from the American Academy and Institute of Arts and Letters, has written over seventeen plays, among them *The Cocktail Hour, Love Letters, The Dining Room, Another Antigone, Scenes from American Life, Children, Richard Cory, The Wayside Motor Inn, The Middle Ages, What I Did Last Summer, The Golden Age, Sweet Sue,* and *The Fourth Wall*. He is also the author of three novels: *The Snow Ball, The Gospel According to Joe,* and *Entertaining Strangers*. Gurney won a Drama Desk Award in 1971, a Rockefeller Award in 1977, a National Endowment Award in 1982 and a Lucille Lortel Award in 1989. He is also a member of the Artistic Board of Playwrights Horizons in New York City, where many of his works have been performed.

ALSO BY A. R. GURNEY

Published by the Penguin Group
Penguin Books USA Inc., 375 Hudson Street,
New York, New York 10014, U.S.A.

Love Letters *and* Two Other Plays: The Golden Age *and* What I Did Last Summer

The Cocktail Hour *and* Two Other Plays: The Perfect Party *and* Another Antigone

A. R. GURNEY

LATER LIFE

THE FIRESIDE THEATRE
GARDEN CITY, NEW YORK

Later Life copyright © A. R. Gurney, 1994
All rights reserved

CAUTION: Professionals and amateurs are hereby warned that LATER LIFE is subject to a royalty. It is fully protected under the copyright laws of the United States of America, and of all countries covered by the International Copyright Union (including the Dominion of Canada and the rest of the British Commonwealth), and of all countries covered by the Pan-American Copyright Convention and the Universal Copyright Convention, and of all countries with which the United States has reciprocal copyright relations. All rights, including professional, amateur, motion picture, recitation, lecturing, public reading, radio broadcasting, television, video or sound taping, all other forms of mechanical or electronic reproduction, such as information storage and retrieval systems and photocopying, and the rights of translation into foreign languages, are strictly reserved. Particular emphasis is laid upon the question of readings, permission for which must be secured from the author's agent in writing.

The stage performance rights in LATER LIFE (other than first class rights) are controlled exclusively by the DRAMATISTS PLAY SERVICE, INC., 440 Park Avenue South, New York, N.Y. 10016. No professional or non-professional performance of the play (excluding first class professional performance) may be given without obtaining in advance the written permission of the DRAMATISTS PLAY SERVICE, INC., and paying the requisite fee.

Inquiries concerning all other rights should be addressed to Gilbert Parker, c/o William Morris Agency, Inc., 1350 Avenue of the Americas, New York, N.Y. 10019.

SPECIAL NOTE

All groups receiving permission to produce LATER LIFE, THE SNOW BALL, and THE OLD BOY are required 1) to give credit to the author as sole and exclusive author of the play in all programs distributed in connection with performances of the play and in all instances in which the title of the play appears for purposes of advertising, publicizing or otherwise exploiting the play and/or a production thereof; the name of the author must appear on a separate line, in which no other name appears, immediately beneath the title and in size and prominence of type equal to 50% of the largest, most prominent letter used for the title of the play and 2) to give the following acknowledgment in all programs distributed in connection with performances of the play, on the first page of credits and on all posters in type size not less than 35% of the size of type used for the largest of the author's name:

"Playwrights Horizons, Inc., New York City, produced
'LATER LIFE' Off-Broadway
in 1993."

SPECIAL NOTE ON SONGS AND MUSIC

For performance of such songs and music mentioned in this play as are in copyright, the permission of the copyright owners must be obtained; or other songs and music in the public domain substituted.

Printed in the United States of America
Set in Bembo

Designed by Steven N. Stathakis

Without limiting the rights under copyright reserved above, no part of this publication may be reproduced, stored in or introduced into a retrieval system, or transmitted, in any form, or by any means (electronic, mechanical, photocopying, recording, or otherwise), without the prior written permission of both the copyright owner and the above publisher of this book.

LATER LIFE

LATER LIFE

To Charles Kimbrough

Later Life was first produced at Playwrights Horizons (Don Scardino, artistic director) in New York City on May 23, 1993. It was directed by Don Scardino; the set was by Ben Edwards; the costumes were by Jennifer Von Mayrhauser; the lighting was by Brian MacDevitt; the sound was by Guy Sherman; the wigs were by Daniel Platten; and the production stage manager was Dianne Trulock. The cast was as follows:

AUSTIN   *Charles Kimbrough*
RUTH   *Maureen Anderman*
OTHER MEN   *Anthony Heald*
OTHER WOMEN   *Carole Shelley*

The play moved to the Westside Theatre, where it reopened on August 10, 1993. It was produced there by Stephen Baruch, Richard Frankel, and Thomas Viertel, along with the Shubert Organization. At this theatre, the part of Austin was played by Edmond Genest, followed by Josef Sommer.

CHARACTERS

AUSTIN

RUTH

SALLY
MARION
NANCY } to be played by one actress
ESTHER
JUDITH

JIM
ROY
DUANE } to be played by one actor
TED
WALT

SETTING

The terrace off an apartment in a high-rise building overlooking Boston Harbor. Good outdoor furniture, including a chaise. A hurricane candle and an ashtray on an upstage table. Occasional greenery. Several chrysanthemum plants to suggest the fall. A romantic, starry sky behind.

The play is to be performed without an intermission.

The author is indebted to Henry James.

Before rise:

Elegant music such as Scarlatti or Vivaldi.

At rise:

Evening light, early September.

The music is now heard coming from within, along with sounds of a lively party. The stage is empty. We hear occasional harbor sounds—a buoy bell, a foghorn.

SALLY *comes on, busily. She wears whatever a hostess would wear.*

SALLY (*beckoning toward within*): Come out here, Austin! (*She adjusts a couple of chairs so that they face more toward each other. She speaks more to herself.*) I'm setting the stage here. That's all I can do. Just set the stage. . . . (*Again toward within:*) I said, come on out.

(AUSTIN *comes out, somewhat hesitantly. He is a distinguished, good-looking, middle-aged man, who wears a gray suit, a blue shirt, and a conservative tie. He carries a glass.*)

Now wait here.

AUSTIN: Why should I wait here?

SALLY: So you can talk.

AUSTIN: To you?

SALLY: No, not to me, Austin. I'm much too busy to talk. (*She lights the outdoor candle.*) I want you to talk to *her.*

AUSTIN: Who's "her"?

SALLY: You'll see.

AUSTIN: Oh, Sally . . .

SALLY: No, Austin, it's time you took a chance. I'll go get her. (*She starts back in.*) Now please. Just wait.

AUSTIN (*calling after her*): What do I do while I wait?

SALLY (*adjusting his tie*): You think. You admire the view of Boston Harbor. You examine your immortal soul. I don't care, as long as you wait.

> (*She hurries off.*)
> (AUSTIN *waits, uneasily.*)
> (JIM *comes out. He might wear a beard or a mustache, and is rather scruffily dressed.*)

JIM: I believe this is where people may still smoke.

AUSTIN: I should think so. Yes.

JIM (*going to the ashtray on the table*): That looks very much like an ashtray.

AUSTIN: I guess it is.

JIM (*examining it*): It is indeed. It is definitely an ashtray. (*Holding it up:*) Appealing object, isn't it? Notice the shape.

AUSTIN: Yes.

JIM: Do you suppose there are still people in the world who design ashtrays?

AUSTIN: I imagine there are. . . . In Europe.

JIM (*producing an unopened pack of Marlboros*): Speaking of design, this pack itself also has a subtle appeal. Notice the brightness of the red, the crispness of the lettering, the abstract white mountain peak behind, luring us on.

AUSTIN: Oh, yes. I see.

JIM: Do you realize that at least eighty percent of the price we pay for cigarettes goes for packaging and taxes?

AUSTIN: I didn't know that.

JIM: And with Clinton in, the tax will be substantially higher.

AUSTIN: Yes, well, Clinton . . .

JIM (*opening the pack carefully*): On the other hand, the packaging is important. There is nothing sweeter than the smell of fresh tobacco. (*He holds it out to* AUSTIN.) Smell.

AUSTIN: Oh, well . . .

JIM: No, I'm serious. Smell.

(AUSTIN *takes the pack and sniffs.*)

You see?

AUSTIN (*handing it back*): It's quite pleasant. . . .

JIM: Pleasant? That is the aroma of rural America. There is a hint of the Virginia planter in that, and the stolid yeomen farmers of the North Carolina plains, coupled with the personal cologne of Senator Jesse Helms.

AUSTIN: Ha ha.

JIM (*beginning to tap out a cigarette*): This is also a pleasant process. Tapping the first one out. Gently coaxing him away from his companions. All the time knowing that there are nineteen others, waiting patiently for their turn. . . . Oh. Excuse me. Want one? (*He offers* AUSTIN *one.*)

AUSTIN: No thanks.

JIM: Sure?

AUSTIN: Positive.

JIM: You don't smoke?

AUSTIN: No.

JIM: Never did?

AUSTIN: No.

JIM: Not even when everyone else did?

AUSTIN: No.

JIM: Never even tried it?

AUSTIN: Oh, well, I suppose behind the barn. . . .

JIM (*taking a cigarette for himself*): That's too bad. You've missed something in life. Smoking is one of the great pleasures of the phenomenal world. It's the closest we come to heaven on earth—particularly now it's forbidden fruit. (*He takes out a lighter.*) It adds depth and dimension to whatever we say or do. Oh, I know, I know: it corrupts children, it exploits the Third World, it is gross, addictive, and unnecessary. It is an image of capitalism in its last, most self-destructive stages. But . . . (*He puts the cigarette in his mouth, lights the lighter, holds it almost to his cigarette.*) It is also a gesture of freedom in an absurd universe. (*He suddenly snaps the lighter shut.*) And I'm giving it up.

AUSTIN: Are you serious?

JIM: I am. I have made the decision. That's why I'm behaving like such an asshole.

AUSTIN: Oh, I wouldn't say that.

JIM: No, really. I've given it up before, of course, but tonight is the big night. I bought this fresh pack, and came out here because this time I'm trying to confront temptation. I am shaking hands with the devil. I am deliberately immersing myself in the dangerous element.

AUSTIN: Do you teach around here?

JIM: That's not important. What I do—or rather, what I did—was smoke. I was an existential smoker. I smoked, therefore I was.

AUSTIN: I'm sure you teach.

JIM: No, I smoked. I am what they call a recovering nicoholic. Or what *I* call tobacco-challenged. My days were comforted by this pleasant haze. My nights were highlighted by this glowing ash. Cigarettes provided the only significant punctuation in the sprawling, ungrammatical sentences which composed my life. And therefore, even though I was an outcast, a pariah, a scapegoat, I wore my badge of shame with honor. I flaunted it. Hey, it was my scarlet letter. (*He returns the cigarette to the pack.*)

AUSTIN (*laughing*): Come on. Where do you teach? Harvard? B.U.? M.I.T.? Where?

JIM: All right. I confess. I have taught. Philosophy. At Brandeis. They made me take early retirement last year. They claimed I slept with too many students.

AUSTIN: Oh, now . . .

JIM: But I think the real reason was I smoked.

AUSTIN: All right now. Enough's enough.

JIM: I agree. You must forgive me. (*Caressing the pack of cigarettes:*) But you see, I'm saying goodbye to a lifelong companion. Nothing becomes it like the leaving thereof. (*He sniffs it longingly.*) Yet it's an agonizing decision! All decisions are, at our age. For us, there's no turning back. Younger people can change their minds, change their lives, that's fine, they have a lifetime ahead of them to change again. But for us who have had a whiff of the grave—it all boils down to our last chance.

(SALLY *comes back out, with* RUTH *in tow.* RUTH *is a lovely woman, who wears a simple, slightly artsy dress. She carries a glass of white wine.*)

SALLY: Here we are! . . . Now go away, Jimmy. (*To* AUSTIN:) Has he been boring you about smoking?

JIM: I've given it up, Sal.

SALLY: So you said last week.

JIM: This time I am.

SALLY: Then go away and *do* it, Jimmy. I want these two people to talk.

JIM (*to* AUSTIN, *as he leaves*): Next time you see me, I'll be a shadow of my former self. I'll be a negative entity, defined not by what I am but by what I am not. You will perceive and know me simply as a Nonsmoker.

SALLY: Just go, Jimmy. Please.

JIM: All right. But I hope you'll remember me for when I came . . . and saw . . . and conquered the habit.

(JIM *goes. The party sounds continue within.*)

SALLY: He's a nice man, but he smokes.

AUSTIN: Give him a chance, Sally.

SALLY: I'm giving *you* a chance, Austin. . . . This is Ruth. . . . And Ruth, this is Austin. . . .

AUSTIN (*extending his hand*): How do you do.

RUTH: Hello.

(*They shake hands.*)

SALLY: Ruth's from out of town.

AUSTIN: Then welcome to Boston.

SALLY (*looking from one to the other*): And?

RUTH: He doesn't remember.

SALLY (*to* AUSTIN): You don't remember Ruth?

AUSTIN: Should I?

SALLY: She remembers you.

RUTH: I do. I definitely do.

SALLY: She said she noticed you the minute you walked into the room.

RUTH: Oh, not the *minute* . . .

SALLY (*to* AUSTIN): Did you notice *her*?

AUSTIN (*with a polite bow*): I certainly do now.

RUTH: I told you he wouldn't remember.

SALLY: Well, then *get* him to.

RUTH: I'll try.

SALLY: And let me break the ice here: Austin, I told Ruth you were divorced, and I'm hereby telling you that Ruth is.

RUTH: Not divorced. Separated.

SALLY (*coming down to* RUTH): Judith said you were divorced.

RUTH: Judith thinks I should be.

SALLY (*recovering her equanimity*): Well, the point is, here you are. Now make the most of it.

(*She goes.*)
(*Pause.*)

AUSTIN: We've met?

RUTH: We have.

AUSTIN: When?

RUTH: Think back.

AUSTIN: To when?

RUTH: Just think.

AUSTIN: I'm thinking. . . . (*He looks at her carefully.*) Ruth, eh?

RUTH: Ruth.

AUSTIN: What's your last name?

RUTH: That won't help.

AUSTIN: What was your last name when we met?

RUTH: You never knew my last name.

AUSTIN: I just knew Ruth.

RUTH: That's all you knew.

(*Pause.*)

AUSTIN: Were you married?

RUTH: Then?

AUSTIN: When we met.

RUTH: Oh, no.

AUSTIN: Was I?

RUTH: No.

AUSTIN: Ah. Then we're talking about way back.

RUTH: Way, way back.

AUSTIN: Were we in college?

RUTH: No.

AUSTIN: School, then.

RUTH: I doubt if we would have met either at school or at college.

AUSTIN: Why not?

RUTH: Not everybody in the world went to Groton and Harvard.

AUSTIN: So I have learned in the course of my life. . . .

(RUTH *laughs*.)

I feel like a fool.

RUTH: Why?

AUSTIN: An attractive woman came into my life. And I don't remember.

RUTH: My hair was different then.

AUSTIN: Still. This is embarrassing.

RUTH: You want a hint?

AUSTIN: No, I should get it on my own. . . . (*He looks at her carefully.*) There's something. . . . Goddammit, I pride myself on my memory! I can remember when I was two and a half years old.

RUTH: You cannot.

AUSTIN: I can. I can remember still being in my crib.

RUTH: I doubt that.

AUSTIN: No, really. I can remember. . . .

RUTH: What?

AUSTIN: It's a little racy.

RUTH: Tell me.

AUSTIN: I don't know you well enough.

RUTH: Oh, come on. We're both adults.

AUSTIN: I can remember being wakened in my crib by a strange sound. A kind of soft, rustling sound. And— (*He stops.*) Never mind.

RUTH: Go on. You can't stop now.

AUSTIN: It was my nurse—we had this young nurse. I specifically remember seeing her through the bars of my crib. Standing by the window. In the moonlight. Naked. Stroking her body. And I lay there watching her.

RUTH: Through the bars of your crib.

AUSTIN: Through the bars of my crib.

(*Pause.*)

RUTH: Austin.

AUSTIN: What?

RUTH (*melodramatically*): I am that nurse.

AUSTIN: No.

RUTH: No. Just kidding.

(*They both laugh.*)

No, we met after college.

AUSTIN: After college, but before I was married.

RUTH: And before I was.

AUSTIN: You are presenting a rather narrow window of opportunity, madam.

RUTH: I know it.

AUSTIN: I got married soon after college.

RUTH: As did I, sir. As did I.

AUSTIN: So we are talking about a moment in our lives when we were both . . . what? Relatively free and clear.

RUTH: That's what we were. Relatively. Free and clear.

AUSTIN: Those moments are rare.

RUTH: They certainly are.

(*Sounds of the party within.*)
(MARION *comes out, gray-haired and maternal.*)

MARION (*looking out and around*): Oh! . . . Ah! . . . Oh! . . . Now that is what I call a beautiful view! (*She calls toward offstage.*) Roy, just come out here and look at this view! You can see all of Boston Harbor!

(ROY *comes out hesitatingly. He is grim and cold.*)

See, sweetheart? There's the U.S.S. *Constitution* right over there, with the lights on the rigging! (*To* RUTH:) Old Ironsides! (*Looking out:*) And behind it is Revere Beach! And that must be Salem to the north. And those little lights way off to the right might even be Cape Cod. (*To* AUSTIN:) Excuse me, sir. You look like one of those people who know everything.

AUSTIN: Oh, I'd hardly say that.

MARION: Do you at least know Boston?

AUSTIN: I've lived here all my life.

MARION: Well, then, could you tell me: are those little lights Cape Cod?

AUSTIN: They are indeed. They're the lights of Provincetown.

MARION: And I imagine on the other side of the building you can see the Old North Church, and the Charles River, and the spires of Harvard.

AUSTIN: I imagine you can.

MARION (*taking his arm*): Oh, isn't that spectacular! Look, Roy! Just look! It's all here, sweetie!

(ROY *moves up reluctantly.* MARION *turns to* AUSTIN.)

And he wants to leave it.

ROY: I have to leave it.

MARION: You don't have to at all.

ROY (*to* RUTH): I have to move south.

MARION (*to* AUSTIN): He doesn't have to at all.

ROY (*to* RUTH): The weather is getting me down.

MARION: Now you'll hear about his arthritis.

ROY: I've got terrible arthritis.

MARION: It's all in his mind.

ROY: Notice how cold it is. Early September and you can already feel the chill.

MARION (*to* RUTH): Are you cold?

ROY: Of course she's cold.

MARION: *I'm* not cold at all.

ROY: Let the lady talk. (*To* RUTH:) Are you cold?

RUTH (*with a glance at* AUSTIN): Actually, since we've been out here, we've been getting warmer.

MARION (*to* ROY): You see? It's all in your mind.

ROY (*to* RUTH): Last night it got down to fifty-eight.

MARION (*to* AUSTIN): He talks about temperatures all day long. He wanders around the house tapping thermometers.

ROY (*to* RUTH): I've got arthritis in my knees and hips.

MARION (*to* AUSTIN): Will he take a pill? Will he submit to medication? He will not.

ROY: I was once a runner.

MARION: He's never gotten over it.

ROY: I ran the marathon six times.

MARION: I had to line up the whole family on Commonwealth Avenue every Patriots' Day, and cheer him on toward the Prudential Center.

RUTH: What's Patriots' Day?

AUSTIN (*to* RUTH): Ah. It's our own special holiday. It commemorates Paul Revere's ride to Lexington and Concord. " 'Twas the eighteenth of April, in 'seventy-five—"

MARION (*taking over*): "—And hardly a man who is now alive / Who remembers that famous day and year. . . ."

AUSTIN: Good for you. (*To* RUTH:) These days we celebrate it by running a marathon.

RUTH: Sounds very Boston.

AUSTIN: What do you mean?

RUTH: Everyone running madly toward an insurance building.

AUSTIN (*laughing*): Ah, well, I look at it in another way. We celebrate a Greek marathon because we're the Athens of America.

MARION: Exactly! (*To* ROY:) Listen to this man, Roy. He knows. He's chosen to live here all his life. (*To* AUSTIN:) I wish you'd tell my husband why.

RUTH: Yes. I'd be interested in that, too.

AUSTIN: Chosen to live here? Oh, I don't think I ever *chose*. I was born here, I've lived here, I've been here, and now I don't think I could be anywhere else.

MARION: That's because it's the most civilized city in America.

RUTH (*To* AUSTIN): Do you agree?

AUSTIN (*bowing to* MARION): I'd never disagree with such a passionate advocate.

MARION: Thank you, sir.

ROY (*to* RUTH): I did the marathon of seventy-eight under four hours.

MARION: She doesn't *care*, Roy.

ROY: I came in six hundred and seventy-nine out of over fifteen thousand registered contenders.

MARION: Roy . . .

ROY: Now I'm paying for it. Now it's bone against bone. You should see the x-rays.

MARION (*to* AUSTIN): He's found this retirement community in Florida.

ROY (*to* RUTH): It has its own golf course.

MARION: It looks like a concentration camp.

ROY: Oh, for chrissake!

MARION: It has gates! It has guards!

ROY: At least I can stagger around a golf course.

MARION (*to* AUSTIN): It's an armed camp. He's moving me from Athens to Sparta.

ROY: At least I'll get exercise. At least I'll be out of doors.

MARION: We'd be leaving our friends, leaving our children . . .

ROY: A man's got to do something. A man can't just sit and grow old.

MARION: Leaving our grandchildren . . .

ROY: Brace yourselves. Here it comes. I sense it coming.

MARION: We have two grandchildren living almost around the corner. (*She opens her purse.*)

ROY: Here come the pictures.

MARION: I just want them to see.

ROY (*walking away*): Watch it. Sometimes she flashes her pornography collection.

MARION (*sitting down, getting out the pictures*): That's not even funny, Roy! (*She shows* RUTH *a picture.*) There. See? Could you walk away from that?

(AUSTIN *stops walking away.*)

I mean, don't you just want to take a bite out of them?

ROY (*warming his hands at the outdoor candle*): They're not interested, Marion.

MARION: You mean *you're* not interested, Roy. (*To the others:*) He doesn't like his grandchildren.

ROY (*coming down*): I like it when they come, I like it when they go.

MARION: He won't help, he won't pitch in.

ROY: You have the instinct. I don't.

MARION: Everyone has the instinct.

ROY (*with increasing passion*): I have the instinct to migrate south! I have the instinct to land on a golf course!

MARION: See what I'm up against?

ROY: And now I have the instinct to go inside and get warm!

MARION (*with equal passion*): All I want to do is enjoy my own grandchildren!

ROY: You can enjoy them after I'm dead!

(*He goes in.*)
(*An embarrassing pause.*)

MARION: Why have I followed that man around all my life? Answer me that. Do I have to follow him to Florida, just so *he* can follow a golf ball around? (*She slaps her knees.*) My knees are fine! There's nothing wrong with *my* knees. (*She gets up, starts out.*) One of these days he might look over his shoulder and find *me* running my *own* marathon! Right back here. To this wonderful city. And that perfectly marvelous view!

(*She looks at the view one more time, glances at* AUSTIN *and* RUTH, *and then hurries in after* ROY.)

Roy! . . . Roy!

(*And she is off.*)
(*Pause.*)

AUSTIN (*to* RUTH): That view may change.

RUTH: Oh yes?

AUSTIN: There is a group—a consortium—which has approached our bank with a serious proposal to turn Boston Harbor into—what is the expression?—a "theme park." Can you imagine? One of the great natural harbors of the New World! These old wharves have already given way to condominia, such as this one. And soon, if the developers get their way, that lovely string of islands, which once guided the great sailing vessels into port, will be transformed into fake Indian encampments and phony Pilgrim villages. We'll be invaded by tourists from all over multicultural America, lining up to see daily reenactments of the Boston Tea Party and the landing at Plymouth Rock.

RUTH: And are you fighting it, tooth and nail?

AUSTIN: No.

RUTH: No?

AUSTIN: How can you fight history?

RUTH: I suppose by making it.

AUSTIN: Yes, well, apparently you and I made our own private chronicle some time ago, didn't we? Where were we?

RUTH: B.M.

AUSTIN: I beg your pardon.

RUTH: Before Marriage.

AUSTIN: Ah.

RUTH: But after college.

AUSTIN: Was I working then?

RUTH: No.

AUSTIN: No?

RUTH: You claimed you were working. But you were really playing.

AUSTIN: You mean, I was taking time out from my obligations at home to serve my country abroad.

RUTH: I mean, you were a very handsome young naval officer steaming around the Mediterranean.

AUSTIN: You mean, I was defending Western democracy against the constant threat of Soviet domination.

RUTH: I mean, you were living it up, while you had the chance.

AUSTIN: Hmmm.

RUTH: Yes. Hmmm. (*Pause.* RUTH *hums a tune: "Isle of Capri."*)

AUSTIN: Is that a hint?

RUTH: Of course. (*She hums a few more bars.*)

AUSTIN: Sing the words.

RUTH: You sing them. (*She hums again.*)

AUSTIN (*singing*): " 'Twas on the Isle of Tra-Lee—"

RUTH: Wrong.

AUSTIN: " 'Twas on the Isle of Capri that I met her . . ."

RUTH: Right.

AUSTIN: The Isle of Capri?

RUTH: Right.

AUSTIN: Let's see . . . Capri . . . Our ship came into Naples . . . and a bunch of us had liberty . . . so we took a boat out to the Isle of Capri.

RUTH: And?

AUSTIN: And . . . God, let's see . . . we saw the Blue Grotto, and we took a cable car or something. . . .

RUTH (*singing*): "Funiculì, funiculà . . ."

AUSTIN: We took a funicular up some hill. And there was a restaurant on top. And we had some beers. . . . (*It begins to come back.*) And at the next table was a bunch of American girls who were touring Italy. . . .

RUTH: Marsh Tours. See Italy in ten days. Summer Special for the sisters of Sigma Nu from the University of Southern Illinois.

AUSTIN: I struck up a conversation with a girl named . . . Ruth!

RUTH (*Italian accent*): Bravo!

AUSTIN: Hello, Ruth!

RUTH: Hello, Austin.

(*They shake hands again.*)

AUSTIN: What a memory!

RUTH: For that, at least.

AUSTIN: We got along, didn't we?

RUTH: We did. Immediately.

AUSTIN: I remember cutting you off from the herd—

RUTH: Oh, no. I cut *you* off. From *your* herd.

AUSTIN: Anyway, we ended up out on some terrace . . .

RUTH: Overlooking the Bay of Naples . . .

AUSTIN: Which is one of the great natural harbors of the *Old World*.

RUTH: Sorrento to the south . . .

AUSTIN: Ischia to the north . . .

RUTH: Vesuvius smoking in the distance . . .

AUSTIN: Actually, I think Vesuvius had given up smoking.

RUTH: I suppose it had to. There must have been pressure from the people of Pompeii.

AUSTIN: I should think so.

(*Both laugh.*)
   (*The party within is getting livelier, with livelier music.*)
   (DUANE *sticks his head out. He wears a short-sleeved shirt and high-waisted pants.*)

DUANE: Hi there. I'm Duane.

AUSTIN: Hello, Duane . . .

RUTH: Hello, Duane . . .

AUSTIN: Austin and Ruth.

DUANE: Seem to have lost the wife.

AUSTIN: I don't believe she's here, Duane.

DUANE: Small woman? Maybe a little . . . overemotional? (*He peers over the upstage railing.*) She's been upset lately.

AUSTIN: Oh?

DUANE: Reason is, I don't think she wants me to upgrade.

AUSTIN: Upgrade?

DUANE: I've been shopping around for a new IBM compatible with an Intel 486 processor.

AUSTIN: Ah.

DUANE: I think she'd prefer I stay with my old machine.

AUSTIN: I see.

DUANE: So tonight we meet this VP from Data-Tech out on 128, and the guy's just *bought* one! With a new scanner that would knock your socks off! He starts telling us about it, and my wife just turns tail and walks away.

(RUTH *walks away*.)

AUSTIN: Oh, dear.

DUANE: I keep saying I'll upgrade her, too, if she wants. I'd be glad to upgrade her. I mean, she's still using DOS 2.0, if you can believe it.

AUSTIN: Oh.

DUANE: I tell her she's back-spacing herself into the Dark Ages.

AUSTIN: Ah.

DUANE: Well, she's in the files somewhere. I'll just have to search and locate, that's all. I've checked the bar, now I'll check the bathroom. I mean, she may not appreciate a premium machine, but she sure appreciates premium vodka.

AUSTIN: We'll keep an eye out for her, Duane.

DUANE: Thanks, guys. (*He starts out, then stops.*) Say. You folks look like PowerBook users.

AUSTIN: What?

DUANE: Just point and click, am I right?

RUTH: That's one way of putting it.

DUANE: Well, you're way ahead of my wife. She's still hung up on Wordstar 2000. Won't install WordPerfect. Refuses even to touch the mouse!

(DUANE *goes off.*)

AUSTIN (*to* RUTH): Touch the mouse?

RUTH: Skip it.

AUSTIN: Maybe we'd better . . . Let's sail back to the Bay of Naples.

RUTH: Yes. Quickly. Let's.

AUSTIN: Suddenly I want to know . . . Did I . . . ?

RUTH: Did you what?

AUSTIN: Did I kiss you on Capri?

RUTH: Yes, you did.

AUSTIN: I did?

RUTH: Oh, yes. Almost immediately.

AUSTIN: I was a horny bastard.

RUTH: You seemed so. Yes.

AUSTIN: What else did I do?

RUTH: You talked.

AUSTIN: I talked?

RUTH: You said things.

AUSTIN: Did you say things?

RUTH: No. Not really.

AUSTIN: What did you do?

RUTH: I listened.

AUSTIN: I talked, you listened?

RUTH: Primarily.

(*They are sitting down by now.*)

AUSTIN: Was I drunk?

RUTH: A little.

AUSTIN: I used to get smashed whenever I went ashore.

RUTH: Smashed or not, you seemed dead serious.

AUSTIN: About you?

RUTH: About yourself.

AUSTIN: Good God.

RUTH: I don't think I've ever heard anyone else say the things you said. Before or since. That's really why I remembered you.

(*More party sounds; moody jazz music.*)
    (NANCY *comes out, carrying a plate of food and a bottle of beer. She wears slacks and might have a Louise Brooks–style hairdo. She might speak with a Long Island lockjaw accent.*)

NANCY: They have food in there. . . . Don't let me interrupt, but they have food. (*She shows them her plate.*) See? Food. (*She looks at it.*) I think it's food. (*She tastes it.*) Yes. It's definitely food. (*She noisily drags the chaise downstage.*) Don't think I'm antisocial, but someone else is joining me, so I'll sit over here. (*She gets settled.*) Continue your conversation. Don't mind me.

AUSTIN (*to* RUTH): Are you hungry?

RUTH: Not really. Are you?

AUSTIN: Not yet.

RUTH: Why rush for food?

AUSTIN: I agree.

(*Pause.*)

NANCY (*looking at her food*): I don't know what this is exactly. It looks like chicken. Shall I taste it? I'd better taste it. (*She tastes it.*) Yes. This is definitely chicken. In a kind of cream of curry sauce. (*She takes another bite.*) And there's dill in this. Just a tad of dill. It's quite good, actually. I recommend it. (*She begins to eat.*) But please: go on with what you were saying. You both look terribly intense.

AUSTIN (*To* RUTH): How about another drink?

RUTH: No thanks. I'm fine.

AUSTIN: Sure?

RUTH: Absolutely.

AUSTIN: People drink less these days.

(NANCY *is chugalugging her bottle of beer.*)

RUTH: Some people.

(*Pause.*)

NANCY: I don't know where my companion is. We were having a perfectly pleasant conversation, and she said, "Oh, there comes the food. Let's get food," so we got into line, and I thought out here we might be able at least to sit *down*. So here I am. (*She looks off.*) But where is *she*?

AUSTIN: I imagine it's quite crowded in there.

NANCY: It is. It's a mob scene.

RUTH: Maybe your friend got lost in the shuffle.

NANCY: Maybe she wanted to get lost . . . or maybe she wanted *me* to get lost.

AUSTIN: Oh, I doubt that.

NANCY: You never know. People can be very peculiar. It's too bad, though. I thought I was getting on with this one. I thought we clicked.

(AUSTIN *looks at her, is a little taken aback, then turns to* RUTH.)

AUSTIN: Are you cold?

RUTH: Oh, no.

AUSTIN: It's not summer anymore. That's why people are staying indoors.

RUTH: I think it's fine.

AUSTIN: Tell me if you're cold. We'll go in.

RUTH: Do you want to go in?

AUSTIN: No, I don't. Do you?

RUTH: No, I really don't.

AUSTIN: If we went in, we might get lost in the shuffle, too.

RUTH: Exactly.

(*Pause.*)

NANCY (*eating something else*): Now *this* is a vegetable casserole. That's all this is. Zucchini, of course. (*She sticks her tongue out.*)

And tomatoes. A bean or two. It's all right. It'll pass. C minus, I'd say. If that. (*She takes a bite of bread.*) But the bread is good. Very chewy. It would be better with butter. No one serves butter in Boston anymore. But still, it's fine. (*She continues to eat.*)

AUSTIN (*to* RUTH): So. You were saying . . .

RUTH (*softly*): Wait.

AUSTIN: We were talking about—

RUTH (*putting a hand on his arm*): Just wait.

AUSTIN: I'm always waiting.

RUTH: I know.

AUSTIN: You *know*?

RUTH: That's one of the things you told me on Capri.

AUSTIN: I told you that?

RUTH: Ssshh.

(NANCY *is now looking at them.*)
  (*Pause.*)

NANCY (*crumpling up her napkin*): Well, that's that. (*She puts her plate aside, gets up.*) That is definitely that. That was very pleasant. Of course, it might have been slightly *more* pleasant if I hadn't had to eat alone. I mean, she was right behind me in the line. And then she just disappears. It was really very rude. (*She opens her compact, puts on lipstick.*) Are you two married?

AUSTIN: Oh, no. God, no. No.

NANCY: I thought you might be married and were having a fight.

AUSTIN: No, no.

NANCY: Are you lovers, then?

RUTH: No.

NANCY: Be frank.

RUTH: No, we're not.

NANCY (*hovering over them*): Then you're arranging an affair, aren't you? You're arranging an assignation.

AUSTIN: No, we're not doing that, either. I don't think we're doing that. (*To* RUTH:) Are we doing that?

RUTH: I don't know. Are we?

AUSTIN: I think we're just talking.

RUTH: That's right. That's all. Just talking.

AUSTIN: Just two old friends, catching up.

NANCY (*looking them up and down, then focusing particularly on* RUTH): I see. Well. Life has taught me this: even if the main course is somewhat disappointing, there's always dessert.

(*She goes out.*)
(*Pause.*)

AUSTIN: A rather disconcerting woman.

RUTH: I'll say.

AUSTIN: We might have been a little rude to her.

RUTH: Rude?

AUSTIN: We didn't . . . bring her in.

RUTH: I didn't want to bring her in.

AUSTIN: We should have.

RUTH: Why?

AUSTIN: It was the polite thing to do.

RUTH: Oh, hell.

AUSTIN: I worry about these things.

RUTH: That's because you went to prep school.

AUSTIN: No, not just because of that. I believe in civility.

RUTH: Being from Boston . . .

AUSTIN: Well, I do. The more the world falls apart, the more I believe in it. Some guy elbows ahead of me in a line, I like to bow and say, "Go ahead, sir, if it's that important to you." Treat people with civility and maybe they'll learn to behave that way.

RUTH: It's been my experience that they'll feel guilty and behave worse.

AUSTIN: Well, *I* feel guilty now. Because I wasn't polite.

RUTH: I feel fine.

AUSTIN: You do?

RUTH: Yes, I do. Because we were doing something very rare in this world that is falling apart. We were making a connection. That's something that happens only once in a while, and less and less as we get older, so we shouldn't let anything get in its way.

AUSTIN: Okay, Ruth. I'll buy that. Okay.

(*Sounds of party laughter from within.*)
(DUANE *sticks his head out again.*)

DUANE: Hi there again.

AUSTIN: Hello . . . ah . . .

DUANE: Duane.

AUSTIN: Duane.

RUTH: Duane.

DUANE: Thought you folks should know: I found the wife.

AUSTIN: In the bathroom?

DUANE: In the kitchen. The caterer was feeding her coffee.

AUSTIN: Uh-oh.

DUANE: No, no. Everything's batched and patched. (*He glances off.*) She's right there in the hall, having a quiet conversation with an old friend from Wellesley. (*He waves to her.*)

AUSTIN: I'm glad, Duane.

DUANE: You see, what we did was sit right down at the kitchen table and talk things over.

AUSTIN: Sounds very wise.

DUANE: Sure was. We put our cards on the table. And I suddenly retrieved the fact that today's her birthday!

AUSTIN: Really!

DUANE: No wonder she was upset. There I was, yakking away about the 486, and she just wanted personal recognition.

AUSTIN: Why don't you buy her a present, Duane?

DUANE: Right. Hey, how about a gift certificate to Radio Shack? . . . Just kidding. . . . No, I'm a romantic guy if you push the right buttons. In fact, I already have a present for her.

AUSTIN: Already?

DUANE: What I did was telephone the kids immediately, and tell them to modem into the new twenty-four-hour nationwide home shopping free delivery channel. Tonight, when we get home, my wife is going to find one dozen long-stem red roses waiting in the bedroom, personal note attached.

AUSTIN: That might do it.

DUANE: It sure should. Maybe I'm learning something in my old age. (*Calling off:*) Right, honey? Maybe I'm finally learning that women like to be put in their own special subdirectory! . . . Honey? (*To* AUSTIN *and* RUTH:) Pardon, folks. Once again the wife seems to have scooted off the screen.

(DUANE *goes off.*)

AUSTIN: I have the terrible feeling that our future grandchildren will be able to respond to Duane more than to anyone else at this party.

RUTH: Austin.

AUSTIN: Hmmm?

RUTH: Tell me. Did it ever happen?

AUSTIN: Did what ever happen?

RUTH: What you told me about. On Capri.

AUSTIN: What did I tell you about, on Capri?

RUTH: I guess it never happened.

AUSTIN: You've lost me, Ruth.

RUTH: When we had our long talk, you told me you had this problem.

AUSTIN: I did?

RUTH: You did. You said you had a major problem. That's what I remember most about the whole evening. That's really why I wanted to talk to you again. I had to know how it came out.

AUSTIN: What was my problem?

RUTH: Want me to say it?

AUSTIN: Sure.

RUTH: You won't be embarrassed?

AUSTIN: I hope not.

RUTH: You said—and I can quote you almost exactly—

AUSTIN: After all these years?

RUTH: After all these years. . . . You said that you were sure something terrible was going to happen to you in the course of your life.

AUSTIN: Did I say that?

RUTH: You did.

AUSTIN: Something terrible?

RUTH: That's what you said. You said you were waiting for it to happen. You said you'd already spent most of your life waiting.

AUSTIN: What? All of twenty-two years? Just waiting?

RUTH: You said it again ten minutes ago.

AUSTIN: Oh, well . . .

RUTH: No, but that's what you said. You said that you were sure that sooner or later something awful was going to descend on you and ruin your life forever.

AUSTIN: God. How melodramatic.

RUTH: It didn't seem so, then.

AUSTIN: You took me seriously?

RUTH: Absolutely.

AUSTIN: I must have been bombed out of my mind.

RUTH: I'm not so sure. . . .

AUSTIN: And I must have been trying to snow you.

RUTH: Maybe . . .

AUSTIN: I mean, there we were, on the Isle of Capri, overlooking the Bay of Naples . . . me, ashore on liberty after ten days at sea . . . you, an attractive young girl . . .

RUTH: Thank you.

AUSTIN: I must have been trying to snow the pants off you.

RUTH: Well, if you were, you succeeded.

AUSTIN: I did?

RUTH: You most certainly did. In fact, after we got back to the mainland, I invited you up to my room.

AUSTIN: Come on! Surely I'd remember that!

RUTH: The reason you don't remember it is, you said no.

AUSTIN: I said no?

RUTH: Or rather, no thank you.

AUSTIN: And did I give a reason for saying no thank you?

RUTH: Oh, yes. You said you couldn't get involved, because of your problem.

AUSTIN: What?

RUTH: You said you liked me too much to drag me into it.

AUSTIN: I said that?

RUTH: I swear. You said you liked me very much, you liked me more than anyone you'd ever met, and therefore you had to say goodnight.

(*Pause.*)

AUSTIN: I must have been drunk as a skunk.

RUTH: By then you were sober as a judge.

AUSTIN: Hmmm.

RUTH: So. You gave me a big kiss goodnight and went back to your ship.

AUSTIN: And what did you do?

RUTH: Well, if you remember, everybody else was hanging around the hotel bar, drinking beer. . . .

AUSTIN: Did you do that?

(*Pause.*)

RUTH: No.

AUSTIN: No?

Maureen Anderman *(left)* as Ruth with Charles Kimbrough as Austin.
All photos of the 1993 Playwrights Horizon production © T. Charles Erickson.

Anthony Heald and
Carole Shelley as
Other Men and Other Women.

Charles Kimbrough as Austin.

RUTH: I went out on the town with a friend of yours.

AUSTIN: A friend?

RUTH: Another officer.

AUSTIN: Who?

RUTH: Oh, Lord, I don't remember. I think he had an Irish name.

AUSTIN (*immediately*): Denny Doyle? Assistant gunnery officer on the forward turret?

RUTH: That could have been the one.

AUSTIN: Denny Doyle? That son of a bitch! He's from Boston, too, you know. He came back and ran for the state legislature!

RUTH: I'll bet he won.

AUSTIN: He sure did. He had every cop in South Boston in his hip pocket. . . . Oh, Christ! You did *Naples* with Denny Doyle?

RUTH: I didn't feel like rejoining the "herd."

AUSTIN: That guy was a mover from the word go!

RUTH: He was full of life, I'll say that.

AUSTIN: He was full of bull!

RUTH: Well, he was fun.

AUSTIN: I don't think he ever told me he took you out.

RUTH: I'm glad he didn't.

AUSTIN: He must have thought you were my girl.

RUTH: For a moment there, I thought I was.

AUSTIN (*bowing to her*): I apologize, madam. For turning such a lovely lady down. And leaving her to the lascivious advances of Denny Doyle.

RUTH: Well, you had your reasons.

AUSTIN: Apparently I did.

RUTH: I'll never forget it, though. What you told me. I've met lots of men with lots of lines before and since—but no one ever told me anything like that.

AUSTIN: Some line. What a dumb thing to tell anyone.

RUTH: Oh, no. It worked, in the long run.

AUSTIN: It worked?

RUTH: It's made me think about you ever since.

AUSTIN: Really? More than Denny Doyle?

RUTH: Much more. Particularly when . . .

AUSTIN: When what?

RUTH: When terrible things happened to me.

(*Pause.*)

AUSTIN: *Now* would you like a drink?

RUTH: No thanks.

AUSTIN: Actually, I would.

RUTH: I'll bet you would.

AUSTIN: Shall we go in while I get a drink?

RUTH: You go in, if you want.

AUSTIN: I'm not going to leave you out here alone.

RUTH: Why not?

AUSTIN: It's rude.

RUTH: Oh, nuts to that.

AUSTIN: You're not cold?

RUTH: Not at all.

AUSTIN: Then I'll be back. (*He starts in.*)

RUTH: Austin . . .

(*He stops.*)

How do I know you're not retreating back to your ship?

AUSTIN: Because I'm older now.

RUTH: Which means?

AUSTIN: Which means I learn from my mistakes.

RUTH: That's good to hear.

(AUSTIN *starts in again, then stops.*)

AUSTIN: Will you be here when I get back?

RUTH: Sure. Unless Denny Doyle shows up again.

AUSTIN: He just might. He's now head of the Port Authority, and wild as a Kennedy.

RUTH: Then you better hurry.

AUSTIN: I will. And I'll get us both drinks.

(*He goes.*)

(*Pause.* RUTH *settles onto the chaise, looks out. We hear the party within, with more sentimental music now in the background.*)

(TED *and* ESTHER *come out. They wear bright colors and have southern accents.*)

TED (*to* RUTH): Hi there. We're the McAlisters.

RUTH: Hello, McAlisters.

ESTHER: Ted and Esther.

RUTH: I'm Ruth.

TED (*as they look at the views*): We just moved north six months ago.

ESTHER: Can't you tell from how we talk?

TED: We're trying to make the most of Boston.

ESTHER: It's a fascinating experience.

TED: We thought it would be a stuffy old town.

ESTHER: You know: stuffy New England . . .

TED: But it's not at all.

ESTHER: It's different, it's exciting. No wonder they call it the New Boston.

(*They come down to* RUTH *on the chaise.*)

TED: We're making a point of meeting everyone at this party.

ESTHER: And everyone has a story.

TED: If you can just find out what it is. For example, we met this man, a perfectly ordinary-looking man, who turns out to be a real Indian—

ESTHER: Native American, honey.

TED: That's right. A Tuscarora, actually.

ESTHER: He teaches history at Tufts.

TED: Think of that. A Tuscarora chief. Teaching history at Tufts. And there he was, drinking a dry martini.

ESTHER: Teddy said, "Be careful of the old firewater."

TED: And he laughed.

ESTHER: He did. He laughed.

TED: Oh, yes. And we met a couple who travels to Asia Minor every year.

ESTHER: To do archaeology.

TED: So I said, "Maybe we should all talk Turkey."

ESTHER: They didn't laugh.

TED: He did. She didn't.

ESTHER: Oh, well. She's from Cambridge.

TED: And we met several Jewish people.

ESTHER: They're all so *frank*.

TED: That's because they've suffered throughout history. You'd be frank, too, if you'd suffered throughout history.

ESTHER: Oh, and there's an African-American woman in there. Who writes poetry.

TED: And we met this Hispanic gentleman—

ESTHER: Latino, honey. He prefers Latino. And he wants to—shall I say this, Ted?

TED: Sure, say it, we're among friends.

ESTHER: He says he wants to become a woman.

TED: Said he was seriously thinking about it.

ESTHER: Can you imagine? Of course, they say the Boston doctors are the finest in the world.

TED: He may have been pulling our leg.

ESTHER: I know. But still . . . I mean, ouch.

TED: And we met a woman from Cambodia, and a man from Peru—

ESTHER: He looked like an Astec prince.

TED: Half-Astec, anyway.

(*Both laugh.*)

ESTHER: Anyway, he had a story. Everyone has a story.

TED: What's your story, Ruth?

RUTH: Mine? Oh, gosh. That would take years. Are you prepared to sit down and listen to all three volumes?

(TED *and* ESTHER *immediately pull up chairs.*)

ESTHER: Are you a Bostonian, at least?

TED: At least tell us that.

RUTH: Oh, no. That's the last thing I am. I'm just visiting my friend Judith. She's the Bostonian. She moved specially from New York to play in the symphony.

ESTHER: We *met* her! She plays the viola?

RUTH: That's the one.

TED: We met her! She's a little . . . nervous, isn't she?

RUTH: Oh, she just gets upset when things get out of tune.

TED: She thinks things are out of tune?

RUTH: She sure thinks I am.

ESTHER: Where are you from, Ruth?

RUTH: Originally? Oh, well, I was born in the Midwest, but I've kind of kicked around over the years.

TED: And now?

RUTH: And now you might say I'm circling over Logan Airport. Wondering whether to land.

TED: Do it. Come on in.

ESTHER: It's a real nice place to live.

RUTH: That's what Judith says. She thinks I could use a little stability.

ESTHER: Why?

RUTH: Oh, she thinks I court disaster.

TED: That must mean you're married.

(*Everyone laughs.*)

ESTHER: Are you?

RUTH: Four times.

TED: Hey, we're talking to a veteran here.

RUTH: Twice to the same man.

ESTHER: Oh, my.

RUTH: He was very . . . persuasive. (*Pause.*) Still is.

TED: We're talking to a real veteran here.

RUTH: I was married to my first husband for only seven days.

ESTHER: Mercy! What happened?

RUTH: Bad luck. He was killed in Asia.

ESTHER: A real veteran here. A veteran of foreign wars.

RUTH: Korea. Long after the war. A land mine exploded. And he just happened to be there.

ESTHER: Oh, dear.

RUTH: It was just bad luck, that's all. Just very bad luck.

ESTHER: That's a sad story. But at least it's a story. You see? Everybody has a story.

TED: Any children, Ruth?

RUTH (*after a pause*): One daughter. (*Pause.*) Not by him. (*Pause.*) By my second husband. (*Pause.*) You don't want to hear this.

ESTHER: No, we do, we do.

TED: If you want to tell us.

(*Pause.*)

RUTH: We lost her. (*Pause.*) To leukemia. (*Pause.*) When she was eleven years old.

TED: It must be terrible to lose a child.

ESTHER: It must be the worst thing in the world.

RUTH: It is. It's . . . hell. (*Pause.*) We brought her home. She died at home. That . . . helped.

ESTHER: You and your husband pulled together. . . .

RUTH: Yes, we did. We pulled together. But when she was gone, we had nothing left to . . . pull. So we pulled apart.

ESTHER: Oh, dear.

RUTH: But . . . life goes on.

TED: It does, Ruth. It definitely does.

RUTH: So I married a man of the West.

ESTHER: Number three?

RUTH: And four.

ESTHER: Oh my.

TED: He's a cowboy?

RUTH: He thinks he is. . . . He'd like to be. . . . He drives a Ford Bronco.

TED: At least he buys an American vehicle.

RUTH: Oh, yes. He's very—American.

ESTHER: Do you like the West, Ruth?

RUTH: The answer to that is yes and no. (*Pause.*) I'm a little at sea about that. (*She looks out.*) Maybe I'll find new moorings in Boston Harbor.

ESTHER: We're all wanderers, aren't we?

TED: Ships that pass in the night.

RUTH: Some are. (*She glances off to where* AUSTIN *has gone.*) Some aren't. (*Pause.*) Lord knows I am.

TED: I didn't think we would be. But we are now.

ESTHER: We got sent here from Atlanta by his company.

TED: Out of the blue. Just pick up stakes and go, they said.

ESTHER: We didn't want to go at all.

TED: We thought we'd freeze to death, to begin with.

ESTHER: But finally we just said what the hell.

TED: We held our noses and jumped, and here we are.

ESTHER: We got an apartment on Marlborough Street. . . .

TED: Surrounded by students . . .

ESTHER: And we've taken the Freedom Trail.

TED: And we walk to the Gardner Museum. . . .

ESTHER: And Symphony Hall . . .

TED: And we even got mugged once. . . .

ESTHER: All he took was our Red Sox tickets—

TED: And we're taking a course in Italian at the Harvard Extension—

ESTHER: "Nel mezzo di mia vita . . ."

TED (*quietly, seriously*): That's Dante. "In the middle of my life."

ESTHER (*looking at him tenderly*): Which is the way we feel. In the middle of our lives.

(*They nuzzle each other.*)

TED: I think everyone over fifty should change their life, Ruth.

RUTH: Oh, well. I've done that, all right. That I have definitely done. Trouble is, I keep doing it.

TED: We were in a rut before, I'll tell you that.

ESTHER: We were. Maybe we didn't remarry, but we sure remade our bed.

TED: Now it's more fun sleeping in it.

ESTHER: Oh, now, Ted . . .

TED: The sex has perked way up.

ESTHER: Ted, please . . .

TED (*slyly*): The South shall rise again!

ESTHER: Teddy!

TED: So welcome to Boston, Ruth. It's a great town.

RUTH: I hope you're right.

(AUSTIN *comes back, carrying two drinks in one hand and two plates of food in the other.*)

AUSTIN: I'm back.

RUTH: These are the McAlisters.

TED: Ted and Esther.

AUSTIN (*bowing*): Austin here.

ESTHER (*checking her watch*): Actually, we've got to go.

TED: Right you are. (*To* AUSTIN *and* RUTH:) We made reservations.

ESTHER: There's a place on Route One where you dance.

TED: The old kind of dancing. And not too Lawrence Welky, either.

(*They begin to demonstrate.*)

ESTHER: And the new. We do the new, too.

TED (*demonstrating*): We do disco.

ESTHER (*demonstrating*): We've learned some new moves.

TED: Some students taught us.

RUTH: Sounds like fun.

TED: Say, want to join us?

(RUTH *looks at* AUSTIN.)

AUSTIN: Oh, I don't think so. Not tonight, thanks.

RUTH (*to* TED *and* ESTHER): We haven't seen each other in years, and we're trying to catch up.

AUSTIN: Thank you very much for asking us, though. Thank you.

ESTHER: Next time I want to find out *your* story, Austin.

AUSTIN: I don't have a story.

RUTH: Oh, yes you do.

ESTHER: Of course you do.

TED: Everyone has a story.

RUTH: Austin has a special story.

ESTHER: Well then, get him to tell it.

RUTH: I'm working on that.

TED: Goodbye, you two.

RUTH: Goodbye, McAlisters.

ESTHER: Ciao!

AUSTIN: Goodbye all.

(TED *and* RUTH *go off.*)

That must be what they call the New South.

RUTH: They sure fit into the New Boston.

AUSTIN: I suppose every place is getting pretty much the same these days. Like airports.

RUTH: No. Boston seems different.

AUSTIN: In what way?

RUTH: Well. For one thing, it has you.

AUSTIN (*laughing*): I suppose I am peculiar to these parts. Like baked beans. Though I hope I don't produce the same results. (*He hands her a drink.*) I brought you a vodka and tonic.

RUTH: Thank you.

AUSTIN: Is that what you were drinking?

RUTH: It is now.

AUSTIN: I thought, one last echo of summer.

RUTH: Yes.

AUSTIN: And food. In case you were hungry.

RUTH: Looks delicious.

AUSTIN: There's more sumptuous fare within. But I tried to select what Julia Child tells us is a balanced diet.

(*They sit.*)

RUTH: It all looks fine.

(AUSTIN *takes silverware and a couple of paper napkins out of his pocket.*)

AUSTIN: Silverware . . . and napkins.

RUTH: You're a thoughtful man, Austin.

AUSTIN: Try to be, try to be.

(*Pause.*)
(*Sounds of the party within: quieter talking and more lush, romantic music.*)

RUTH: So.

AUSTIN: So.

RUTH: So it never happened.

AUSTIN: What?

RUTH: The terrible thing.

AUSTIN: Oh, that.

RUTH: It never happened?

AUSTIN: Oh, no. God, no. No.

RUTH: You never made some terrible mistake?

AUSTIN: Not that I know of. No.

RUTH: You were never hit by some awful doom? Things always worked out?

AUSTIN: Absolutely. I mean, I think so. I mean, sure. After the Navy, I came back. Went to the business school. Got a good job with the Bank of Boston. Married. Married the boss's daughter, actually. Two kids. Both educated. Both launched. Both doing well. Can't complain at all.

RUTH: Sally said you were divorced.

AUSTIN: Oh, well, that . . . (*Pause.*) That doesn't . . . She wasn't . . . We weren't . . . (*Pause.*) She fell in love . . . *claimed* she had fallen in love . . . with this . . . this *creep*. I mean, the guy's half her age! . . . So she got her face lifted. Dyed her hair. Does aerobics on demand. . . . I mean, it's pathetic.

RUTH: So that's not the terrible thing?

AUSTIN: Her leaving? Christ, no. That was a good thing. That was the best thing to happen in a long, long time.

RUTH: And nothing else even remotely terrible happened in your life?

AUSTIN: I don't think so. (*He looks for some wood to knock on.*) At least, not yet.

RUTH: You still think something might?

(AUSTIN *looks off into space.*)

    Austin? Hello?

(*He looks at her.*)

    Do you?

(*Pause.*)

AUSTIN: I think it all the time.

RUTH: Really?

AUSTIN: All. The. Time. (*Pause.*) I've been very lucky, you know. Too lucky. From the beginning. It's not fair. Something's bound to . . . (*Pause.*) Want to know something?

RUTH: What?

AUSTIN: I'm on Prozac right now.

RUTH: You are?

AUSTIN: It's a drug. It calms you down.

RUTH: Oh, I know Prozac. I know what it does. And doesn't do.

AUSTIN: I don't tell people I'm on it. But I am.

RUTH: Does it help?

AUSTIN: Yes. . . . No. . . . A little.

RUTH: You shouldn't drink with it.

AUSTIN: I don't. Normally. That was a Perrier I was drinking before.

RUTH: But not now?

AUSTIN: This is a white wine spritzer. Tonight I'm becoming very reckless.

RUTH: Be careful. You might make some terrible mistake.

AUSTIN: Sometimes I wish I would. At least the shoe would drop.

(SALLY *comes out, carrying a sweater. She goes to a light switch.* AUSTIN *gets to his feet.*)

SALLY: Let's have some light on the subject. . . .

(*The outside light comes on.*)

You two seem to be having a perfectly marvelous time.

AUSTIN: We are indeed, Sally.

SALLY (*to* RUTH, *holding out a sweater*): Judith thinks you should wear your sweater.

RUTH: Oh, I'm not cold.

SALLY: Well, Judith thinks you will be.

RUTH: Judith is very solicitous. (*She takes the sweater.*) But I'm perfectly fine. (*She doesn't put it on.*)

SALLY: Did you two ever figure out where you met?

AUSTIN: We did. It was very romantic.

SALLY: Oh, good. But it doesn't have to be. (*She starts gathering up plates.*) I met my sweet, dear Ben after class, in Room 120 of Eliot Hall, when I was auditing his course on Renaissance architecture. He was a superb teacher, he knew everything in the world, but I remember thinking, all during his lectures, "I can teach *him* a thing or two." So I married him, and did.

AUSTIN: I took Ben's course.

SALLY: Everyone took Ben's course. Those were the days when we all tried to learn the same things. (*She starts out, then stops.*) Oh. Which reminds me. There's a little man in there from the Berklee School of Music who has been sniffing around Ben's old Steinway. So when things settle down, we're going to dust it off and try singing some of the old songs. It's probably hopelessly out of tune—*we're* probably hopelessly out of tune—but that's just a risk we'll have to take.

(*She goes out.*)
   (*Pause.*)

RUTH: I like it here. (*She moves upstage, tosses her sweater somewhere.*)

AUSTIN: Boston?

RUTH: My friend Judith says it's very livable. The universities, the music . . .

AUSTIN: My family has had the same two seats at Symphony Hall for four generations.

RUTH: I'm sure.

AUSTIN: Maybe you'd join me some Wednesday evening. If you stay.

RUTH: I'd like that. If I stay. (*Pause.*) One thing that scares me, though. About Boston.

AUSTIN: What's that?

RUTH: Is it a little . . . well, Puritan.

AUSTIN: Whatever that means.

RUTH: Shouldn't do this, have to do that.

AUSTIN: Ah. Yes. Well, some people say there's that.

RUTH: Are they right?

AUSTIN: Puritan? Oh, well. I'm a little . . . close to it. You're probably a better judge.

RUTH: I sense it a little.

AUSTIN: With me?

RUTH: A lot.

(*Pause.*)

AUSTIN: You sound like my shrink.

RUTH: What? You go to a psychiatrist?

AUSTIN: She's the one who prescribed the Prozac.

RUTH: I can't see you with a psychiatrist.

AUSTIN: Neither can I. My kids conned me into it. After the divorce, I happened to be feeling a little . . . well, glum . . . so they gave me two sessions as a Christmas present.

RUTH: Good for them.

AUSTIN: I went so I wouldn't hurt their feelings.

RUTH: And you've stayed so you wouldn't hurt the psychiatrist's feelings.

AUSTIN: Right.

RUTH: God, Austin! You're so polite! When you die, you'll probably say excuse me.

AUSTIN (*laughing*): Maybe so. (*Pause.*) Anyway, it doesn't work. Psychiatry. At least for me. It may work for them—the younger generation. They're so much at home with all that lingo. And they're all so aware of their own feelings. I mean, they strum on their own psyches like guitars. So it probably works for them. I hope it does. After all, their life is ahead of them. But me? Even if I . . . could say . . . even if I found some way of . . . I mean, it's a little late, isn't it?

RUTH: Don't say that. You should never say that.

AUSTIN: Anyway, she hasn't a clue. My psychiatrist. Not a clue. I sit there in this hot room on Copley Square, overlooking Trinity Church, trying to explain. But she hasn't the foggiest. It was all so different. The world I came from. It was a totally different culture. All those . . . surrogates. That's what she calls them. Surrogates breathing down your neck. Nurses. Cooks. Maids. Gardeners. Aunts and uncles. Parents, too, of course. And godparents. Grandparents. *Great*-grandparents, for chrissake. All this pressure. Vertical and horizontal. You were like a fly caught in this very intricate, very complicated spiderweb, and if you struggled, if you made a move, if you even tweaked one strand of the web, why, the spider might . . . (*Pause.*) Anyway, what does she know about a world like that? My shrink. She grew up in a cozy little nuclear family in some kitchen in the Bronx.

RUTH: Nuclear families can be explosive.

AUSTIN: I'd take a good explosion over death by spider. Caught in that web, being systematically wrapped in silk, carefully preserved, until you can't . . . breathe.

RUTH: Oh, now . . .

AUSTIN: Anyway. Puritan. She says I have a Puritan sense of damnation.

RUTH: Oh, yes?

AUSTIN: She says I've inherited a basically Calvinistic perspective from my forefathers in Salem and points north.

RUTH: She says that, does she?

AUSTIN (*settling back on the chaise*): Let's see. How does it go? I've been brought up all my life to think of myself as one of the elect.

RUTH: I see.

AUSTIN: But it's hard to feel elect in a diverse and open-ended democracy. Particularly after George Bush lost the election.

RUTH: So?

AUSTIN: So therefore I'm terrified that I may actually be one of the damned, exiled forever from the community of righteous men and women.

RUTH: Isn't that what they used to call predestination?

AUSTIN: Oh, yes. But she says I'm constantly struggling against it. That's why I'm so polite. I'm trying to propitiate an angry God before He lowers the boom.

RUTH: She's got all the answers, hasn't she? This shrink.

AUSTIN: Oh, well. She went to Radcliffe.

RUTH: And this is what I get if I move to Boston?

AUSTIN: We like patterns here. We like categorizing things. Even our subway system is carefully color-coded. The good guys ride the Red Line.

RUTH: I'm someone who likes to ride anywhere I want.

AUSTIN: Right! And I'm full of bullshit.

RUTH: Austin! Watch your language. They'll sentence you to the ducking stool.

AUSTIN (*laughing*): Hey, this has been good. I feel good now. You've got me talking about these things. I've never done that before.

RUTH: Except with your shrink.

AUSTIN: It's different with you.

RUTH: You never talked about it with your wife?

AUSTIN: Oh, God no. Not with her. Never.

RUTH: Maybe that's why she left.

AUSTIN: Maybe. And maybe that's why you've stayed.

RUTH: Maybe.

AUSTIN: See? I've been snowing you again, just as I did on the Isle of Capri.

RUTH: Oh, is that what you've been doing?

AUSTIN: Has it worked?

RUTH: Oh, yes. It's worked all over again.

AUSTIN: I'm glad.

(*He leans over and kisses her. Behind them the sky is a deep, starry blue, as it was in Naples.*)
   (*Then* WALT *comes out, a little drunk. He wears a navy blazer with a crest on it, and gray flannels.*)

WALT: Austin! Sally tells me you've found a— (*He sees the kiss.*) Whoops. Sorry to interrupt.

(*He goes off.*)

RUTH: Who was that?

AUSTIN: That was my friend Walt.

(WALT *comes back on again.*)

WALT: I heard that. "My friend Walt." I like that. "My friend Walt" . . . (*To* RUTH:) I happen to be his best friend in the entire free world.

AUSTIN: That's true. He is.

WALT: Damn right it's true. (*To* RUTH:) We roomed together at Groton. We had a suite together in Dunster House. I was his best man when he married the lovely Cynthia Drinkwater, of Marblehead, Mass. (*He starts to leave.*) Anything you want to know about this guy, just ask me.

RUTH (*more to* AUSTIN): Is he saved or damned?

WALT (*coming back*): Say again?

RUTH: Is he as good a man as I think he is?

WALT: Better. Austin is—and I now quote from the Groton School yearbook—a prince among men.

AUSTIN: Thanks and goodbye, Walt.

WALT: No, and I'll tell you why, uh . . .

RUTH: Ruth.

WALT: Ruth . . . He hails from one of the finest families in the Greater Boston area. As a banker, he has unimpeachable credentials. As a father, he is fair to a fault. As a husband, he is . . . was . . . gentle, thoughtful, and ultimately forgiving. As a friend, he—

AUSTIN: Cut it out, Walt.

WALT: No, Ruth should know these things. You have been occupying Ruth's time, you have been preventing the rest of us from enjoying the pleasure of Ruth's company, you have obviously been attempting to lure Ruth into your bed—has he been doing that, Ruth?

RUTH: No, he hasn't.

AUSTIN: Yes I have.

RUTH: News to me.

AUSTIN: The Lord moves in strange and devious ways.

WALT: Then Ruth should know what she's in for. So I'll tell you this, Ruth. You are about to go to bed with a great squash player. He'd be nationally ranked in the over-fifties bracket, except he won't play outside of Boston. But put this guy in a squash court and you'll see his true colors.

AUSTIN: Ruth doesn't care about squash.

WALT: I'll bet Ruth does. Because Ruth knows, in her deep heart's core, that good at squash means good in bed.

AUSTIN: Oh, Jesus, Walt. (*He walks upstage.*)

WALT: Would you like me to describe Austin's squash game, Ruth?

AUSTIN: I wish you wouldn't.

RUTH: I wish you would.

WALT: The ayes have it. So. Now the secret to squash—we're talking about squash racquets here—is that you're obliged to be both brutally aggressive and ultimately courteous at the same time. At this, my friend Austin is a master. He will hit a cannonball of a shot right down the rail, and then bow elegantly out of your way so you can hit it back.

RUTH: And what if you don't?

WALT: Then he'll ask if you'd like to play the point over.

AUSTIN: God, Walt.

RUTH: He sounds very special.

WALT: He is, Ruth. Now, as you may know, Boston is a great sports town. We produce champions around here: Ted Williams, Bobby Orr, Larry Bird. And we've also produced Austin.

AUSTIN: This is pitiful . . . pitiful . . .

WALT: No, now listen to me, Ruth. Squash is a very old game. And very British. Henry the Eighth played a version of it at Hampton Court. The British raj played it in India. We Americans picked it up in our Anglophilic days, and naturally made some improvements. But lately the game has come to be considered somewhat obsolete. It is deemed obscure, elitist, and somewhat dangerous. So in an attempt to adjust to the modern world—to accommodate women, to make it more telegenic—they've softened the ball, widened the court, and modified the rules. It is only played the old way in a few old cities: New York, Philadelphia, and of course Boston. And here Austin is still unbeatable. Put him in a clean white box, with thin red lines, and the old rules, and by his squash thou shalt know him.

RUTH: And what happens when he steps out of that clean white box?

WALT: Ah, well. Then he likes to take a cold shower.

AUSTIN (*coming downstage*): Knock it off, Walt! This is embarrassing.

WALT: Okay. Sorry.

RUTH: You like him a lot, don't you, Walt?

WALT: Like him? I love the guy. (*Kissing* AUSTIN *on the cheek:*) I love him a lot.

AUSTIN (*backing away*): Damn it, Walt.

WALT: Hey, it's 1993, man. We can do that now, and not even get called on it.

(*Party sounds.*)

(JUDITH *creeps out self-consciously, beckoning to* RUTH. *She looks like someone who plays in an orchestra. She wears a plain, dark velvet dress and has rather wild, unruly hair. She speaks with a New York accent.*)

JUDITH (*portentously*): Ruth, there's a telephone call for you.

RUTH: For me?

JUDITH: He's tracked you down.

RUTH: Oh. (*To* AUSTIN *and* WALT:) Excuse me. (*She starts in.*)

JUDITH: Ruth . . . I could easily say you're not here.

RUTH: Um . . . well . . . no.

JUDITH: Or Ruth: now listen. I could simply say you don't want to talk to him. Period. I could say that point blank.

RUTH: No. I'll—talk to him. (*She starts in again.*) Where's the phone?

JUDITH: I don't want to tell you.

RUTH: Where is it, Judith?

JUDITH: In Sally's bedroom.

RUTH: I can at least talk to him.

AUSTIN: Will you be back?

RUTH: Of course I'll be back.

JUDITH: Of course she'll be back. (*To* RUTH:) Come back, Ruth. Rejoin the human race.

RUTH: Yes. That's right. . . . (*She starts out again, then stops, returns, puts her arm around* JUDITH. *To* AUSTIN *and* WALT:) Oh. This is *my* friend. Judith.

(*She goes.*)

JUDITH (*shrugging*): Some friend. I shouldn't even have brought the message. I should have walked right into Sally's bedroom and slammed down the phone.

AUSTIN: I'm afraid you have the advantage on this particular subject.

JUDITH: What? Oh. Sorry. That was him.

AUSTIN: Who?

JUDITH: Her husband. He's a deeply flawed person.

AUSTIN: How? How is he flawed?

JUDITH (*looking from one to the other*): Am I among friends here?

WALT: Sure you are.

JUDITH (*after a moment*): He hit her. That's for openers.

AUSTIN: No.

JUDITH: He *hit* her! She had to hit him back!

AUSTIN: Oh, boy.

JUDITH: She told the whole group.

AUSTIN: What group?

JUDITH: I'm sorry. I'm so keyed up I forgot to play the overture. (*She does some breathing exercises.*) We met in this women's group two summers ago at the Aspen Music Festival. My husband and I played Mozart in the morning, and I signed up for assertiveness training in the afternoon. There was Ruth, dealing with her divorce. I thought we were all making great strides, but in the end she went back to her husband.

AUSTIN: So the group didn't help.

JUDITH: It helped me. I decided to leave mine.

AUSTIN: Oh, dear.

JUDITH: I decided he was a weak man.

WALT: Weak—uh—physically?

JUDITH: Weak musically. Weak on Mozart, weak on Mahler, weak even on "Moon River."

AUSTIN: And this—group had a say in all that?

WALT: These women's groups work, man. (*To* JUDITH:) My wife, Ginny, went to one. It improved her net game enormously.

JUDITH (*to* WALT): There you are. They open new horizons. I learned there's more to life than the string section. I'm now seriously involved with a French horn.

AUSTIN: May we talk about Ruth, please.

JUDITH: Ruth? Ruth was unable to release. I mean, the man is a disaster. Once she almost called the police.

WALT: Oh, Christ. One of those.

JUDITH: You got it. One of those. Still, back she goes.

AUSTIN: To where?

JUDITH: Are you ready? Las Vegas.

AUSTIN: Las Vegas?

JUDITH: He likes to live in Las Vegas.

AUSTIN: I'm unfamiliar with Las Vegas.

JUDITH: So am I, and pray to God I remain so. But that's where they live. Furthermore, he's gone through every nickel she's got. She starts this lucrative little art gallery—creates an oasis of civilization out there—and what does he do but bankrupt her.

AUSTIN: Why is she even talking to him, then?

JUDITH (*with an elaborate, complicated, hopeless shrug*): You tell me.

WALT: The guy must have some hold.

JUDITH: Some hammerlock, I call it.

AUSTIN: What does he do in life?

JUDITH: Do? Do? The man gambles. Period. End of sentence.

AUSTIN: Uh-oh.

JUDITH: And to support his habit, he manages a car-rental business.

AUSTIN: Oh, boy. I can tell you, as a banker, that is a very erratic business.

JUDITH: She says he likes all that. He likes being out on a limb.

WALT: Have you met him?

JUDITH: No, thank God. But she showed me his picture. That's another problem. He looks like the Marlboro man.

WALT: Uh-oh. Better load up your six-shooter, Austin.

JUDITH: Please. No macho stuff. Please. It's her choice. She's got to learn to kick the habit.

AUSTIN: Maybe she will.

JUDITH: From your mouth! I mean, the man's a barbarian! Once he grabbed her television and threw it out the window!

AUSTIN: Good Lord.

JUDITH: While she was watching "Jewel in the Crown."

WALT (*to* AUSTIN): There's the bell, buddy.

AUSTIN: What?

WALT: Your serve, man. Time to make your move.

JUDITH: It's time for everyone to make a move. It's time to make a concerted effort.

WALT: Damsel in distress, pal.

JUDITH: Which is why I brought her here tonight. I wanted to show her what civilized life was all about.

WALT: You wanted to show her Austin.

JUDITH: Austin? Austin was just luck. But when she said she *knew* you, Austin, and when Sally said you were *free*, I thought, YES! At least there's *hope*!

AUSTIN: Hey, gang. Don't paint me into a corner here.

JUDITH: All I know is she's a sweet person, and she's had a rough life, and she deserves a better break than she's had so far. . . . Let me see if I can pry her loose from that goddamn telephone!

(*She goes off quickly.*)

WALT: You like her?

AUSTIN: Ruth?

WALT: Of course Ruth.

AUSTIN: I hardly know her.

WALT: She seems like a good gal.

AUSTIN: She's very . . . simpatico.

WALT: You need someone, buddy.

AUSTIN: I've got someone, buddy.

WALT: Who? Your little friend up in Nashua?

AUSTIN: She's there when I need her.

WALT: I'm talking about more than a dirty weekend in New Hampshire, Austin.

AUSTIN: Oh, are you, Walt?

WALT: Give this one a chance.

AUSTIN: I'm not sure what you mean.

WALT: I mean, Ginny and I have tried to fix you up several times. But you gave those ladies short shift, or shrift, or whatever the fuck the expression is.

AUSTIN: Of course I'll give her a chance. I like to think I give everyone a chance. Why wouldn't I give her a chance?

WALT: Because you're acting like a jerk, that's why.

AUSTIN: What is it with you people in this town? Who do you think I am? Some new boy back at boarding school, being set up for the spring dance? I am a divorced man, Walt! I am a father of two grown children! I'll be a *grand*father any day! At our age, we don't just . . . *date* people, Walt. We don't just idly fool around. Every move is a big move. Every decision is a major decision. You ask a woman out, you take her to dinner, that's a statement, Walt. That says something important. Because there's no second chance this time, Walt. This is our last time at bat!

WALT: All the more reason not to be alone.

AUSTIN: And did you ever think, Walt, did you and Ginny ever think that maybe I *like* being alone? Ever think of that? Maybe I've discovered the pleasures of listening to opera while I'm shaving. And *walking* to work through the Commons—rather than riding that damn train! And having a late lunch with a good book at the Union Oyster House! And reading it in bed at night! Maybe I like all that! Maybe I like feeling free to fart!

(RUTH *comes in, carrying dessert and two demitasses.*)

Excuse me, Ruth.

RUTH: No problem.

AUSTIN: I was just letting off a little—steam.

RUTH: Good for you.

WALT: I'll get back to the party.

RUTH: Goodbye, Walt.

WALT: So long, Ruth. I hope we'll meet again.

RUTH: I hope so, too.

(WALT *goes.* RUTH *sets her plates down.*)

I brought dessert.

AUSTIN (*settling at the table*): Very thoughtful.

RUTH: And coffee.

AUSTIN: Decaf, I hope.

RUTH (*sliding him his cup*): What else.

(*They eat, brownies or something.*)

Mmmm.

AUSTIN: A little rich, isn't it?

RUTH: Well, we deserve it. We were so healthy with the main course.

AUSTIN: Right. In Boston, they'd say we're getting our just desserts.

(RUTH *gives him a weak smile.*)
   (*Pause.*)

Everything all right, by the way?

RUTH: With the telephone call?

AUSTIN: Judith told us who it was.

(*Pause.*)

RUTH: He's at the . . . what is it? The Skyway Lounge, out at the airport.

AUSTIN: What? He's there?

RUTH: He's there.

AUSTIN: And?

RUTH: He wants me to join him.

AUSTIN: When?

RUTH: Now. Right now.

AUSTIN: But you're here.

RUTH: That's right. I'm here. Which is what I said. I said I'm having a very good time right here.

AUSTIN: What did he say to that?

RUTH: He said he could give me a better one, right there.

AUSTIN: Could he?

RUTH: He can be . . . fun.

AUSTIN: Did you tell him about me?

RUTH: No.

AUSTIN: Why not?

RUTH: He might have shown up with a baseball bat.

AUSTIN: I could have dealt with that.

RUTH: Oh, yes? With your squash racquet.

AUSTIN: I would have done something.

RUTH (*touching him*): I know you would have, Austin. (*She gets up.*) I just don't want you to, that's all. (*She looks out.*) He's got two tickets on tonight's red-eye back west. First class. And he wants to order a bottle of champagne to drink while we wait.

AUSTIN: Champagne? At an airport bar?

RUTH: He knows I like it. (*Pause.*) First class, too. He knows I'm a sucker for that. (*Pause.*) And he'll charge everything to *my* credit card.

AUSTIN: Sounds like a nice guy.

RUTH: Oh, he . . . has his problems.

AUSTIN: Sure sounds like it.

RUTH: Of course we all do, don't we?

AUSTIN: Ouch.

RUTH: No, but I mean *we* do. Lord knows I do, too.

AUSTIN: Name one.

RUTH: Him.

AUSTIN: Okay.

RUTH: He's not good for me.

AUSTIN: That's an understatement.

RUTH: But he has some redeeming social virtues.

AUSTIN: Such as?

RUTH: Well . . . for one thing, he loves me.

AUSTIN: Oh, sure.

RUTH: He does. . . . He's never traded me in for some young bimbo. He's never taken me for granted. He loves me. . . . I walk out, I leave him, I say this is it, and what does he do? He telephones all over the country till he finds out where I am. Then he grabs a flight to Boston. Calls me here. Offers me champagne. And begs me to come back. . . . He loves me.

AUSTIN: How can he love you if he hits you?

RUTH: He doesn't hit me.

AUSTIN: I hear he does.

RUTH (*more to herself*): Judith! . . . (*To* AUSTIN:) Once, maybe.

AUSTIN: Once is enough.

RUTH: By mistake.

AUSTIN: Oh, Ruth.

RUTH: It was by *mistake*, Austin!

AUSTIN: Some mistake. That's a big mistake.

RUTH: Sometimes he gets . . . carried away.

AUSTIN: Yes, well, that's not love in my book.

RUTH: Oh, really?

AUSTIN: That has nothing to do with love. Rape, violence, things of that kind—I'm sorry, they elude me. They totally elude me. If that's love, then I'm afraid I know nothing about it.

(*She looks at him as if for the first time.*)
   (*Pause.*)
   (*Sounds of people singing around a piano come from within:*

>   "Oh, we ain't got a barrel of money,
>   Days may be cloudy or sunny,
>   But we'll travel along, singing a song
>   Side by side.")

AUSTIN: Well. How about a song at twilight?

RUTH: Maybe it's better if I just . . . (*She makes a move to go.*)

AUSTIN (*getting in her way*): Ruth.

(*She stops.*)

> Tell you what. We'll go to the Ritz Bar, you and I. It's a very pleasant, very quiet place. And *I'll* buy you champagne. And I promise you it will be a better brand than what your Marlboro man comes up with, out at the airport. And I'll pay for it *myself.*

RUTH: Austin . . .

AUSTIN: No, and I'll tell you something else. After we've had champagne, we'll go to my place. If you'd like.

RUTH: Oh, Austin . . .

AUSTIN: No, now I don't want you to feel obligated in any way. But I have a very nice apartment on Beacon Street, and we can walk there, right down Arlington Street from the Ritz. And I have a guest room, Ruth. It's a nice room. With its own bath. I keep it for the kids. You can sleep there, if you prefer. I'll even lend you a pair of decent pajamas.

RUTH: Decent pajamas . . .

AUSTIN: No, now wait. If, when we're there, you'd like to . . . to join me in my room, if you'd care to slip into my bed, naturally I'd like that very much. Very much indeed. But you wouldn't have to. Either way, you'd be most welcome. And if things worked out, why we might . . . we might make things more permanent . . . I mean, it's a thought, at least. And if they don't—well, hell, you should always feel free to leave any time you want.

RUTH: Oh, well . . .

AUSTIN: I mean, we obviously get along. That's obvious. We did on Capri and we do now. Hey, come to think of it, this is a second chance, isn't it? We're back where we were, but this time we're getting a second chance. (*Pause.*) So. What do you say?

RUTH (*kissing him*): Oh, Austin. Austin from Boston. You're such a good man.

(*She starts out.*)
(*The singing continues within.*)

AUSTIN: Where are you going?

RUTH: I don't want to tell you.

AUSTIN: To him?

RUTH: I think so. Yes.

AUSTIN: Why?

RUTH: Why?

AUSTIN: Why him and not me?

RUTH: Oh, dear.

AUSTIN: How can you love that guy?

RUTH: If you don't know, I can't tell you.

AUSTIN (*turning away from her*): You don't think I'm attractive?

RUTH: I think you're one of the most attractive men I've ever met.

AUSTIN: Then it must be my problem.

RUTH: Yes.

AUSTIN: You think it's a crock of shit!

RUTH: No! Not at all. No! I take it very seriously. I take it more seriously than you do.

AUSTIN: You think something terrible is going to happen to me?

RUTH: I think it already has.

AUSTIN: When?

RUTH: I don't know.

AUSTIN: Where?

RUTH: I don't know that either.

AUSTIN: But you think I'm damned into outer darkness?

RUTH: I do. I really do.

AUSTIN: But you won't tell me why.

RUTH: I can't.

AUSTIN: Why not?

RUTH: It's too painful, Austin.

AUSTIN: Do you think I'll ever find out?

RUTH: Oh, I hope not.

AUSTIN: Why?

RUTH: Because you'll go through absolute hell.

AUSTIN: You mean I'll weep and wail and gnash my teeth?

RUTH: I don't think so, Austin. No. I think you'll clear your throat, and square your shoulders, and straighten your tie—

and stand there quietly and take it. That's the hellish part. (*She looks at him feelingly.*) I've got to dash.

(SALLY *enters.*)

Oh, Sally . . . Goodbye . . .

(RUTH *goes quickly.*)
   (*Singing offstage:*

> "The bells are ringing
> For me and my gal,
> The birds are singing
> For me and my gal . . .")

SALLY (*looking after* RUTH): That was a little abrupt.

AUSTIN: She was in a hurry.

SALLY: She certainly was.

AUSTIN: She asked me to thank you for her. She said she had a wonderful time.

SALLY: You're lying, Austin. (*She kisses him on the cheek.*) But you're also very thoughtful and polite. Now if I were you I'd call her up at Judith's, first thing in the morning.

AUSTIN: She's going back to her husband. Tonight.

SALLY: Oh, no.

AUSTIN: Flying back to Las Vegas.

SALLY: No.

AUSTIN: That's what she's choosing to do.

SALLY: I hear he's bad news.

AUSTIN: How could she go back to a guy like that?

SALLY: Maybe she hopes he'll change.

AUSTIN: People don't change, Sally.

SALLY: Maybe they do in Las Vegas.

AUSTIN: Not at our age. We are who we are, only more so.

SALLY: No, Austin. No. I can't agree with that. No. If that were true, I'd still be rattling around Ben's house on Brattle Street, having tea with his colleagues, talking about his books. But I sold the house, Austin, soon after he died. And I gave his books to the Widener. And I moved down here to the harbor, so I could live a different life, with different people, who talk about different things.

AUSTIN: Different they are, Sally. I'll say that.

SALLY: And they keep me *alive!* . . . Oh, Austin, give it a try. Why not go after her?

AUSTIN: Sally . . .

SALLY: I mean it. She can't have gone that far! (*She sees the sweater.*) Look! She even left her sweater! You see? You're in luck! She's even given you a good excuse! Take it to her! Right now! Please!

AUSTIN: Sally, I'm not going to scamper off to some airport bar to deliver some sweater. . . . She can come back any time she wants.

SALLY: Maybe she *wants* to be swept off her feet!

AUSTIN: I'm a little old to be sweeping people off their feet, Sally. Just a little too old for that.

SALLY: Oh, Austin, you're hopeless. (*She begins to clean up the dessert plates.*) Well. Come join the party. We found *The Fireside Songbook* tucked away in the piano bench, and after we've gone through that, there's talk of rolling back the rug and doing some serious dancing!

(*Within, they are now singing:*

> "*In a cavern, in a canyon,
> Excavating for a mine . . .*")

(JIM *comes out, lighting his cigarette.*)

JIM: I'm sorry. I'm afraid I have to smoke again.

SALLY: At least you tried, Jimmy.

JIM (*his hand shaking as he lights up*): I went almost the whole evening smoke-free, but now look at me, puffing like a chimney.

SALLY: Well, try again tomorrow.

JIM: Right. (*Sitting down, inhaling deeply:*) Meanwhile, gather ye tumors while ye may . . .

(*The singing continues:*

> "*Oh my darlin', oh my darlin',
> Oh my darlin' Clementine . . .*")

I was fine till we started in on that fucking song. It made me think of a cat I had. (*To* SALLY:) Remember my cat, Sal? Clementine?

SALLY (*standing behind him*): Of course I remember Clementine.

JIM (*to* AUSTIN): But it isn't really the cat at all. It's the association with my friend Dalton. (*To* SALLY:) Remember Dalton, Sal?

SALLY: I remember him well. I liked Dalton.

JIM (*to* AUSTIN): I had a friend named Dalton, and we'd put our cat in the car, and sing to her, driving down to Provincetown. Have you ever sung to a cat?

AUSTIN: Can't say that I have.

SALLY (*stroking* JIM*'s hair*): My poor dear Ben loved music.

JIM (*putting out his cigarette*): I'd take the melody, he'd take the harmony. We were fantastic!

SALLY: Ben played all the old songs on that piano. Sigmund Romberg, Rodgers and Hart . . .

JIM (*starting to cry*): Oh, boy. Now look at me. Now I'm starting to cry. . . .

SALLY (*holding him*): Now, Jimmy. Now, now.

JIM: Shit. I'm going to pieces here. I'm totally falling apart.

(*He breaks down, cries unabashedly.* AUSTIN *stares at him, almost hypnotized.*)

Why are you staring? I'm just a sentimental old fag who smokes.

SALLY: Let's go in, Jimmy. It's cold out here.

JIM (*pulling himself together*): You're right. I'm embarrassing you, Sal, in front of your guest. (*He blows his nose, gets up.*)

SALLY (*pulling the chaise back to where it was*): Austin understands, don't you, Austin? (*She hands him Ruth's sweater.*)

AUSTIN (*taking the sweater*): Oh, yes.

SALLY: Everyone in the world loves *something*. Am I right, Austin?

AUSTIN: Oh, yes . . . yes . . .

JIM (*taking off the dessert plates and coffee cups*): Still, it's terrible to let go that way. . . .

(*He goes.*)

SALLY (*To* JIM, *as he goes*): Think how much more terrible it would be if you couldn't! (*She blows out the candle, starts out.*) Coming, Austin?

AUSTIN: In a minute.

(SALLY *goes, turning off the terrace light.*)
(AUSTIN *stands, clutching Ruth's sweater, lit only by the shaft of light coming from indoors. He takes a deep breath, clears his throat, squares his shoulders, straightens his tie, and looks longingly toward the life within, as the lights fade and the singing ends:*

"*Thou art lost and gone forever,
Oh my darlin' Clementine.*")

(*Slow fade.*)